José I. Arocha

THE PRINCIPLES OF SICAMOR

FOR YOUR GROWTH JOURNEY

Special thanks to my dear friend Stephen R. Wiffen, MA (Cantab), for his unconditional help in proofreading this book.

Scriptures quotations are taken from:
[a] The Holy Bible, Catholic Edition, Good News Translation, Today's English Version – Second Edition © 1976, 1979, 1992 American Bible Society
[b] Christian Community Bible, Catholic Pastoral Edition, © Bernardo Hurault, 2016

First self-published in December 2019
Cover photo: Jose I. Arocha, Church of the Holy Family, Singapore
Back photo: Jose I. Arocha, Church of the Holy Family Singapore
Illustrations: Jose I. Arocha
ISBN: 978-981-14-3302-3 (Paperback)
ISBN: 978-981-14-3303-0 (E-book)

To my wife Sonely... With infinite love.

God bless you always.

AUTHOR'S NOTE

We all want to achieve goals in life, academically, professionally, personally, socially, etc. We may set up those goals at an early age or later in life, but we all want to have goals because that make us feel that we have a purpose in life.

Those goals could be big or small. It does not matter because, regardless, achieving those goals allow us to impact positively our lives and those of others. Whatever the positive impact is, we feel we have accomplished something and that makes us feel good about ourselves. Such an impact can just be on a personal level, as in achieving a university diploma or getting married and having children who could carry on our legacy. It could also be on a social scale, like becoming a doctor, an owner of a successful business, a musician, or a writer. Whatever walk of life we take, we all have goals and we all have the capacity to fulfil them.

However, on the way, there will be distractions, temptations, and trial and tribulations that may delay, if not divert, our path towards reaching our goals. Even worse, those can direct us to a path of perdition. Indeed, we will be exposed to the influence from the "world" offering us indulgences and enticing on us to try all sorts of experiences, perhaps someone telling us that gambling is an "opportunity", that smoking is "cool", or that promiscuous sex is "freedom". Some even fall into that trap, convinced that it is one way to "treat" their sorrows, sadness, frustrations, anger, and the like.

But even if we have a minimum of wisdom that allows us to differentiate between good and evil, the seemingly never-ending advance of technology, which exposes us to copious information and ways of communication at almost the speed of light, drowns us with more things than we can handle, and that prevents us in making wise and timely decisions. And this will cause us to go through trials and tribulations, being much more than what we can possibly cope with.

No matter what, we will all go through challenging times and events, and we won't have the option to prevent many of them. It's life. However, we can reduce them by filling our life with blessings that provide us with joy; which, consequently, leaves less time for curses that only produce misery. It is therefore necessary to reinforce some of life's principles that surely will lead to that end. This is the intention of the principles explained in this manual.

Other books by the author:

Sicamor – For Your Growth Journey

This book narrates Sicamor's adventures in his search for wisdom and his journey will bring about unexpected rewards. Find out more at www.kingsicamor.com

CONTENTS

"I have now given you the choice between the blessing and the curse. When all these things have happened to you, and you are living among the nations where the Lord your God has scattered you, you will remember the choice I gave you."

Deuteronomy 30: 1 [a]

INTRODUCTION

"Tree that grows crooked its trunk never straightens."

We all have, most probably, received lots of love, advice, modelling, and education from our parents and teachers. So, why do some of us still struggle throughout our life? If not on a continuous basis, at least during some periods of our growth journey?

We can indeed overcome the obstacles we may find on the way, if we have the necessary strengths and preparation. But we can't do this alone. The reality is that depending only on ourselves, we won't get very far; depending only on our strengths, we won't get anything done. We need heavenly, as well as earthly, help. And some wisdom.

When we fail at something that we thought we were prepared for, we realize that we are still weak and that we need to learn more. But if we have some wisdom, we will not become demoralized and we will move on. Certainly, we can have the necessary strengths to face any situation in life, if we know our weaknesses.

God will present us with countless opportunities to achieve everything we strive for.

He also gave us free will to decide whether we take an opportunity or not. But every opportunity will present challenges as well, but that should not demoralize us either. Taking those opportunities will bear fruit and surely not only for ourselves. We are part of a family, a society, a country and of a planet, and all can benefit from our correct behaviour and by the benevolent harvest that we produce.

It is true that everyone is unique, with his own thoughts, feelings, and behaviour, not moulded only by one's genetics, but also by the teachings from the surrounding circumstances in which we grew up, the relationships around us, and the experiences that we go through during our growth journey. But, regardless, if we have wisdom, we will not deviate from the right path, the one that is lit up, the one that leads us to life; a life that will bear fruit.

As we have free will, the choice between life and death is ours.

> "Life and death are set before man: whichever a
> man prefers will be given him."
> *Sirach 15:17* [b]

OUR CHALLENGES TODAY

Every time we meet someone, it gives us the chance to learn something from him or her, and the opportunity that this person also learns something from us. On each interaction, we take one step forward on our growth journey; our journey to a fruitful life. Therefore, we do need that contact; we do need that human encounter. But, sadly, we are losing it. Why? Because it seems it is not necessary anymore. Everything has been made so uncomplicated for us; so convenient that we can do so many things... without leaving or being away from home.

Studying and working from home is encouraged more and more. Homework is done online, so students don't need notebooks and pencil cases anymore, while keeping their school bags light. And by employees working from home, companies can save money on rental space, air conditioning, and transport allowances.

Eating a "take-away" food at home without cooking, and still taste a huge variety of dishes and at an affordable price, is increasingly becoming a way of life. And while we are at it, we sit comfortably on our couch to watch a blockbuster movie on an extremely high-resolution TV set, in addition of other kinds of entertainment. Long gone are those times when we played games with real friends at the back of our houses, in the town square, or on the streets. Now, we can play soccer on a video-game without even moving our legs and feet.

Consulting a doctor, a lawyer, an expert on any subject, or seeking any information or advice on whatever subject we can think of, is now achieved through a couple of strokes of our fingers on the keyboard; no longer any need to go out. Google knows everything. And we can talk and see our friends, for hours every day as we wish... each one of us sitting or lying on a sofa in our own home.

Very convenient life, indeed, and millions of people revel in. It all really sounds perfect, but it would be better if not for the fake news, misleading information, ambiguous messages, inaccurate data, and deceitful headlines that we receive constantly through the internet. So fake sometimes, that even the pictures of the people claiming responsibility for many of those "messages" are also fake... pictures of people that don't exist and have never existed. Now, it doesn't sound so good anymore, does it?

Facebook, Twitter, WhatsApp, and so many platforms make you truly think that you have "friends". But you don't really know anyone through a screen. It is a huge risk, and we may end up listening to people that may be up to something sinister, that goes totally against our own values and beliefs.

Times also keep changing fast. The childhood of our grandparents was not that different from that of our great-grandparents. Perhaps, the childhood of our parents compared to that of our grandparents were not so very different either. But definitely we cannot say that about our own childhood compared to that of our parents'. The massive technological, social, and cultural advances, especially during the last 20-30 years, have created such a generational gap among the living generations so vast that, in some cases, it's possibly insurmountable.

The larger the generational gap, the more difficult it is for parents to understand their children, and certainly vice versa. The kids won't talk to their parents anymore, much less to listen to their advice; they would rather listen to their friends and peers... and anything sprouting up from the internet. Parents realize they know less and less, while their teenager children think they know everything. Parents cannot cope with the times, thinking that "any time in the past was better," while their children think they are the generation living the best of times.

Last but not least, we live in a constant war against evil. Temptation and curses abound, making it harder to secure a shield of blessings for ourselves. The devil is loose out there indeed, seducing us to fall into temptation.

> "Be sober and vigilant. Your opponent, the devil,
> is prowling around like a roaring lion looking for
> someone to devour."
> *1 Peter 5:8* [b]

Our integrity is being compromised daily. We need to grow strong and to be blessed, to help us walk through our growth journey safe and sound, so we live a fruitful life.

WELCOME!
TO RICHNESS!
TO FREEDOM!
TO POWER!
TO FAME!
TO FREE-WORRY LIFE!
TO PLEASURE!

GROWTH JOURNEY PRINCIPLES

Jesus told us to carry our cross and to follow him. He didn't mean it for just a while, a day, or a month. He meant it for life. Yes. And, for many, it will take a while to realize that we all carry a cross and that we will be carrying it for life... That is, until our death. And while we carry it, we will fall, for sure more than three times, but that shouldn't make us deviate from our journey.

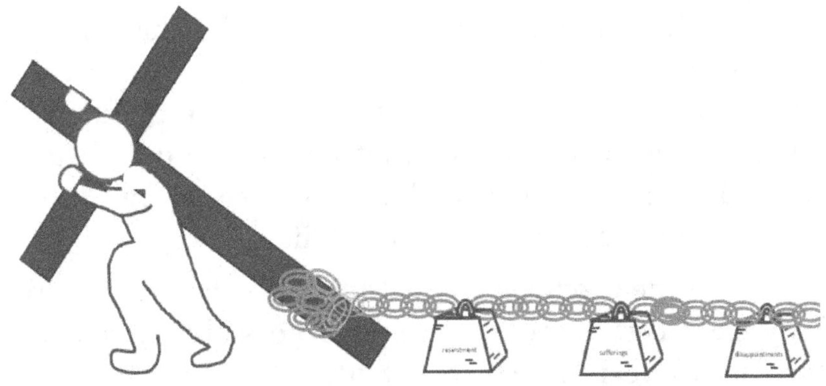

Our crosses are all different, in size, in weight, in type, and they will not stay the same throughout our lives. Most likely, our crosses will become heavier with the passing of time; that is to say, through the passage of life. And it can become heavier because of all the worries, sufferings, disappointments, addictions, sorrows, set-backs... all tribulations that, for sure, we will encounter during our growth journey. These will accumulate, becoming chained onto our crosses.

If you think that only people with disabilities, either physical, mental, or emotional, are carrying a heavy cross, think again. We will all get sick; we all will lose someone close to us; we will be heartbroken; we will fail at a task, a test, or a project; we may go bankrupt; we will hurt and make someone suffer; we will feel ashamed; we will suffer injustice; and so on.

Certainly, many of those events will be life-changing, and some in a dramatic way. Regardless, life-changing or not, those events will only keep adding weight to our crosses and when a pile of them load up, our crosses can build up into a very heavy burden; so heavy, that we may not be able to move forward, or at least not at the desired speed and direction. And we cannot escape... it is part of life.

But the good news is that there are three things we can do. We can keep our cross as light as possible; we can also become stronger to carry it; or both.

Keeping tribulations at bay

There is nothing we can do to avoid tribulations completely during our lives. Many tribulations happen beyond our control. We may see our parents or close friends pass away. Someone may hurt us; or we may hurt someone unintentionally. We are not in control of natural disasters that may hit someone we love or even ourselves, or of a severe economic downturn. We may even lose our job, or be cheated by someone. So, there will always be some painful incident that cannot be controlled.

On the other hand, there are also many other life situations that we can control, at least to a certain degree. An easy way to illustrate this statement has to do with our health. If we eat what we should eat; if we don't participate in dangerous activities; if we get enough sleep and exercise routinely, we may be preventing potential health hazards from eventually appearing, which means fewer tribulations. Many situations can be controlled, if we behave righteously and consciously.

It is, indeed, poor behaviour that can cause many of the tribulations, which, consciously or not, will become chained to our cross. And we may still think that these afflictions will get chained only to our individual crosses. No, it will impact others. Taking the example above, not taking care of our own health and getting sick will also affect our parents, siblings, and friends. Resources, hospital care, and medicines are consumed, all of which are being paid by a lot of people, who we don't even know, through taxes. Similar rationale can be said if we hurt someone physically, if we fall into corruption, or if we go to prison, just to mention a few other tough situations that will bring us tribulations of many kinds.

And then, there are other situations that sometimes are not so clear to spot so easily by people around us. For example, our heart may be aching for something we didn't mean to say, or didn't say; or something we did, or didn't do.

Or, perhaps, someone else did or said something hurtful to us, or didn't do or didn't say what we were expecting. There will be always sorrows... Weight to carry.

In Paradise, there were no tribulations, until Adan and Eve sinned. Now, we all have to live with them. But God still gave us intelligence and conscience, along with free will, to reduce some of the disappointments, sorrows, heart-aches... and many other tribulations.

Keeping our cross light

First, we need to understand that our behaviour is a product of our attitudes to situations that we encounter in life. And our attitudes are driven by our wishes, which are powered by our feelings, which in turn are born from our thoughts. There are many experts in psychology and cognitive behaviour who can elucidate on this subject in greater depth, but the point to highlight is that all those thoughts, feelings, wishes, attitudes, and behaviours can be driven by two supernatural powers, totally opposed to each other. One will pour out blessings on us; the other, curses.

There is a huge difference between a blessing and a curse. A fundamental one; when someone blesses us, it is God giving us His blessings. It is all goodness. When someone curses us, the devil is behind it. It is all evil. He wants us to carry a very heavy cross, so we don't move, we don't grow, and we don't get closer to God. And he will then be stalking us throughout our whole life.

The other big difference between them is that blessings are reducing the weight of our cross, while curses are increasing its weight. All that as a consequence of adding or decreasing grievances and sorrows.

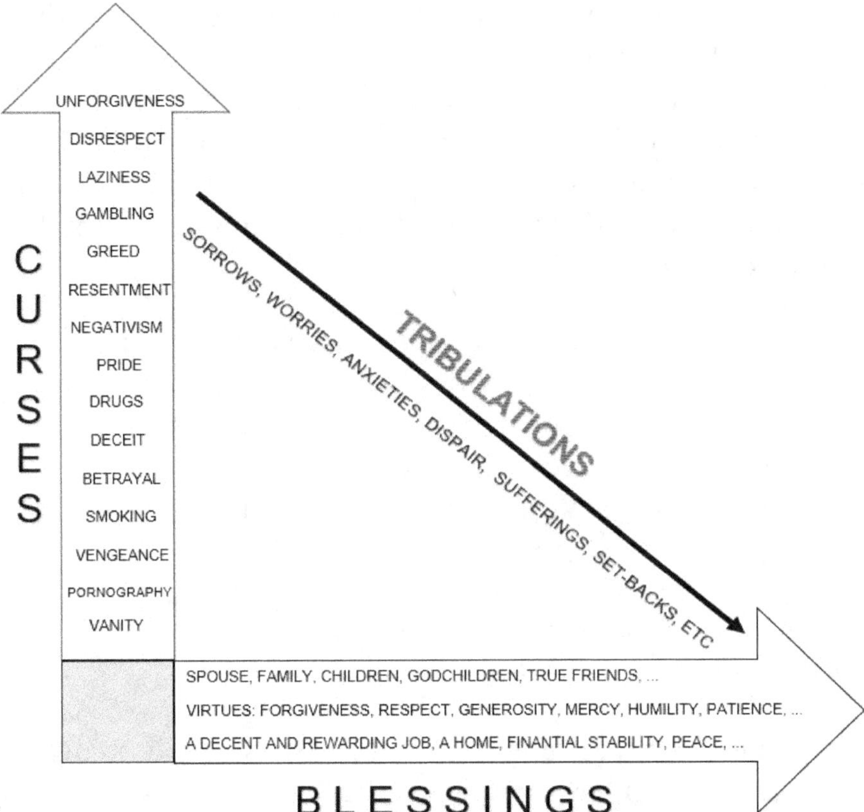

The more the blessings, the fewer the tribulations, and with fewer tribulations, a lighter cross. With a light cross to carry, our growth journey will be more peaceful, rewarding, and fruitful. We all want to carry a light cross.

Blessings

"God blessed them saying: 'Be fruitful and
increase in number, fill the waters of the sea; and
let the birds increase on the earth'."
Genesis 1:22 [b]

We are here to be blessed; all of us, without discriminating anyone. When blessed, we'll pour out the fruits of goodness to all humanity, leading us to a fruitful life; we will be impacting positively everybody and everything that surround us. But most importantly, the blessed person is the one who obeys and follows God, and rejects all temptation and wickedness of the devil.

> "Happy are those who reject the advice of evil
> people, who do not follow the example of sinners
> or join those who have no use for God. Instead,
> they find joy in obeying the Law of the Lord, and
> they study it day and night. They are like trees that
> grow beside a stream, that bear fruit at the right
> time, and shoes leaves do not dry up. They
> succeed in everything they do."
> *Psalm 1:1-3* [a]

Blessings are not only the virtues, good manners, charitable acts and everything else that we are capable to give by following the teachings of God, but also His gifts: family, children, our home, a job, financial stability, a peaceful country.

But we need to give in order to receive.

> "Those who are generous increase their riches;
> others are misers and impoverish themselves. The
> warmhearted soul will prosper; he who waters will
> himself be watered."
> *Proverbs 11:24-25* [b]

Curses

We are not here to be cursed. Yet, life could be filled with temptation, bad influences, and dark desires that will make us behave in a way that we feel awful and unworthy... at least.

A curse will prevent you from growing spiritually, mentally, and even physically. Everything you do may fail, since your behaviour will be wrong, erratic, and senseless.

Curses are not only vices, like those related to drugs, alcohol, or gambling. Curses are also those ill-intentioned feelings, like envy, unforgiveness, and vengeance. Curses are also what paralyzes you, like pessimism, negativism, and sleaziness.

A person that is cursed will have a life filled with tribulations, which ultimately can destroy him.

> "All these curses shall fall upon you, pursue you
> and oppress you until of you perish, for you did
> not listen to the voice of Yahweh, your God, or
> obey the commandments and the norms which he
> gave you."
> *Deuteronomy 28:45* [b]

Becoming stronger

Our thoughts, feelings, wishes, attitudes, and behaviours can then be driven by either blessings or by curses. The key is to know which is which. In most cases, we can identify both at the same level, which means that by choosing one, the other is automatically excluded. For example, if we choose to forgive -a blessing-, we will not allow mercilessness -a curse-, to appear. By choosing a blessing, there will be no room for the curse.

So, by cultivating and filling our life with blessings, we don't only keep our crosses light, but also we become stronger to face upcoming difficulties and challenges, no matter how great or severe these could be. But filling it up with curses can only bring us unhappiness, conflict, struggles, loneliness, prison, hate, indifference, or worse; in addition to an empty, dry, and fruitless life. And someone going through that will have a very vulnerable integrity, being almost impossible to maintain it.

Integrity

Integrity requires that our thoughts, feelings, wishes, attitudes, and behaviours are all synchronized and aligned, meaning that we behave the way we think, that we walk the talk. This is only one side. On the other side, integrity requires that we also behave according to solid and unbreakable values, and by exercising consistently and continuously the blessings we've received.

The principles that are developed next in this book are to provide guidance and insights for a life of ever-growing blessings, and for a growth journey that can bring us happiness, peace, success, prosperity, freedom, and love... in addition to an abundance of accomplishments and fruits along the way.

In the following chapters, we will be discussing those insights, summarized in ten principles that should help us go through a rewarding and fruitful growth journey, with minimal suffering.

The ten Sicamor's Growth Journey principles:

1. Growth starts within us
2. Identify our values
3. Don't let paradigms twist our values
4. Get advice
5. Better safe than sorry
6. Compare to the best
7. Focus on the goal
8. Get to it… act!
9. Make positive impact on others
10. Review yourself constantly

FIRST PRINCIPLE

GROWTH STARTS WITHIN US

"Why, then, do you look at the speck in your
brother's eyes and pay no attention to the log in
your own eye."
Mathew 7:3 [a]

We easily blame and judge others and when we judge someone, we do it based on our beliefs, circumstances, experience, and knowledge. We see in the other person a reflection of our thoughts, feelings, wishes, attitudes, and behaviours. Being mindful of that, we need to look to our own core, into ourselves first, and open up our hearts and minds to receive blessings. From there, our growth starts.

"Our judgment is frequently influenced by our
personal feelings, and it is very easy to fail in right
judgment when we are inspired by private
motives."
Thomas A Kempis in 'The Imitation of Christ'
Penguin Books.

Myself

We arrive into this world pure, at the image and likeness of God, with only the original sin. We begin learning from the very first moment we are fed. Our learning is continuous and unstoppable.

Every day we learn something, especially in this era where information disseminates so fast and deep, readily available with just the touch of our fingers' tips. Modern technology exposes us to all kind of influences or compelling arguments that will, eventually, impact the kind of life we are living and the one we will live.

But it is still up to us whether we receive either blessings or curses.

> "I have now given you the choice between the
> blessing and the curse. When all these things have
> happened to you, and you are living among the
> nations where the Lord your God has scattered
> you, you will remember the choice I gave you."
> *Deuteronomy 30: 1 [a]*

Since we don't live as hermits, hopefully, we must keep in mind that we are not alone and we must acknowledge the presence of other people; people that surround us all the time, from our families, our school or work place, or on the street. All occupying imaginary circles that surround us, the nucleus. Circles that could represent the different levels in which we live and interact, and that ultimately impact our own life and world; circles having their own set of characteristics, demands, offerings... and influence.

My family

The very first circle around us is, or should be, our family. That is, our parents, siblings, and relatives. They will fill our first years of our growth journey with love and care. We, in return, will model them; we will adopt their habits; we will follow their teachings and believe in their beliefs; and so on. Indeed, family is the most important part of our "humanity" during the first few years of our lives. A lot of values are instilled in us then.

We, as children, may not have even realized what we were, subconsciously, absorbing at that time; but today, it may be a good day to remember...

My school, my workplace

Later, a few years down the road, the time at school and the workplace comes to us. Now, we leave home and we will spend most of our time away from home. We start listening to teachers, instructors, mentors, coaches, and tutors. Each one of them eager to provide us with a wide variety of information. It is a little bit scary, considering we are still very vulnerable, but we must take every opportunity to gain the knowledge that school and work-place provide, while getting other values that come along.

> "Unhappy are those who put no value on wisdom
> and instruction, their hope is vain, their efforts
> useless, their work without profit."
> *Wisdom 3:11* [b]

My social circles

Next in line, while growing up at a significant pace and at some point in parallel to school, are our social circles. Long gone are the days when parents knew all of their children's friends and their parents, and their addresses. Nowadays, those social relationships are catapulted by the internet and all its associated social media; this is where it really becomes important that we remain vigilant and alert, very crucial in order to stay on the right path.

The influence from virtual "friends" and the access to all kinds of evil become stronger and more frequent, profuse, and relevant. Exposure to pornography, violence, racism, unnatural ideas, etc. is an evil attack to our integrity, without realizing that, in many cases, the devil is behind it all. There is no worse enemy than the one we don't know about and we can't see. To fight evil, we need to know the enemy and we can only fight it with blessings.

My country

Another important source of influence on us is the society or country where we live. A society has a profusion of policies and rules that are necessary for the harmonious, safety, progress, and well-being of its members. We need the rule of law for all of us to live in a just and stable society. Obeying the rules, or not, will affect our behaviour, which in turn will add to our blessings... or curses.

My planet

And finally comes our planet, not often thought about by many. We love to spend a day on a clean beach or to enjoy a walk in the forest. That is probably the extent of the interaction with mother earth for many. Understandably, on top of our worries and workload, we don't want to add any more. Ozone layer depletion, plastic waste in the oceans, deforestation of the Amazon jungle... Who cares? Well... We should.

Growth starts within us

Since an early age, we are like an absorbent sponge,

but, as for any sponge, we can absorb pure water as well as vinegar. When we reach adulthood and we are more mature, the influence from other people becomes less and less significant, and hopefully by then, we should have already grown in blessings, sitting deep inside our hearts and minds... But not curses. So, all throughout our growth journey, we need to pay attention to what we hear, what we see, what we learn, and process all that virtuously. We ought to become wiser, so we can discern with foresight.

Growth starts within us. We need to be responsible, not only for what we allow to enter into our bodies and minds, but also for what we give to others and to society; and even to the planet. We can, indeed, become the teachers, the models, and the suppliers of blessings, which is a blessing in itself. But for that to happen, we need to open up, work on our values, get good advice, and start making a positive impact on others. The growth journey must start within ourselves. Our purpose in life is to do wonderful things. We only need to start accumulating blessings.

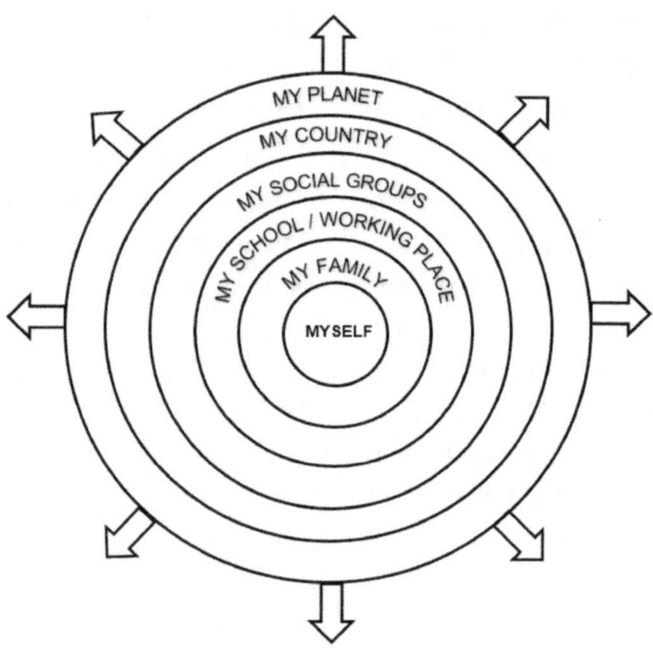

MY PLANET
MY COUNTRY
MY SOCIAL GROUPS
MY SCHOOL / WORKING PLACE
MY FAMILY
MYSELF

SECOND PRINCIPLE

IDENTIFYING YOUR VALUES

All the blessings we may think of: humility, family, generosity, obedience, loyalty, wealth, a good job, or responsibility will only flourish and grow righteously if we have a solid set of values. Those values are always to be placed upfront, and allow them to drive our thoughts, feelings, wishes, attitudes, and behaviours.

Each one of us values something. In fact, we value many things, and we ought to discover what they are. Simply, ask yourself:

'What do I value the most?'

Identify it and whatever you value and care for will open up the door to blessings. By knowing your values, you can start firmly your growth journey in the right direction.

Fundamental and pivot values

Let's first acknowledge our fundamental values. Those are the basic and central ones. These should be related to ourselves, the family, the school or occupation, the social life, the country, and the planet; your surrounding circles. And within each one of those circles, a number of pivot values must also be identified and developed, because they support the fundamental values.

Values, either fundamental or pivot, are instilled in us since our childhood and throughout our growth journey. They will be influenced by the information received from many sources, including our parents, friends, strangers, the ignorant, the expert, and, yes, ill-motivated people; and by using different means: direct and indirect conversation, the daily paper, magazines, books, the radio and television, and the internet. All of that information impacting us at different times and places.

Such information will drill our minds and our souls, sometimes so deep that we will live with it for the rest of our lives, sometimes stubbornly. So, why not fill our minds and souls with elements that will allow us to live a fruitful life? Well, those elements are blessings.

Values regarding ourselves as individuals

We all hope to live a life full of happiness, peace, success, prosperity, rewards, freedom, and love. That is, of course, if we value ourselves, and the fundamental value of ourselves is our life. From here, we identify the pivot values; those that will support our fundamental value... our life. So, we can ask ourselves: 'What exactly do we value in our life?'

You could start with the most important one for you. Is it health? Is it wealth? Independence? If it is health, do you value the spiritual, the physical, or mental health as all being the same? You ought to discover which ones and set those as your pivotal foundations for yourself.

It is also true that our main pivot values may change as we age. Is "having fun", a value during your youth, when you may be forgetting your purity, health, faith, image, instruction, or true friendship?

Values regarding the family

The family is the very basis of any society, so the values to strengthen it are no less important than the individual ones.

It is well known that the devil aims all its evil and malefic power to destroy families. And the individual members of a destroyed family become hurt, doubtful, and vulnerable, making them, thus, an easy prey to fall into curses, promptly becoming both resentful and vengeful. "In the union we find strength," a wise man once said, and a united family, with strong values, can help a weak, doubting, stranded family member.

Of course, each family is different. Its members' backgrounds, habits, and beliefs may differ from another family. But there are some core pivot values on which all families can sustain their very truth of their existence. We may think that sharing the faith is one pivot value needed to grow within our families. Indeed, it is. It may also be keeping harmony within. What else?

It is truly at home, within the family nucleus, where all the values, virtues, and good manners are first taught. The teachings and modelling, that our parents and other members of the family give us, should surely contribute to us continuing unto our next stage in life on two feet.

Values regarding the school, the job

At school is when we open ourselves up to the world. It is the time of our lives when we become people with a life of our own. And another set of values will grow and solidify. We may be too young to understand the whole concept and purpose, but strong values can be identified here as well.

What are those values? Perhaps it is time, one of the most precious resources we have, not only now, but forever... Because time is life.

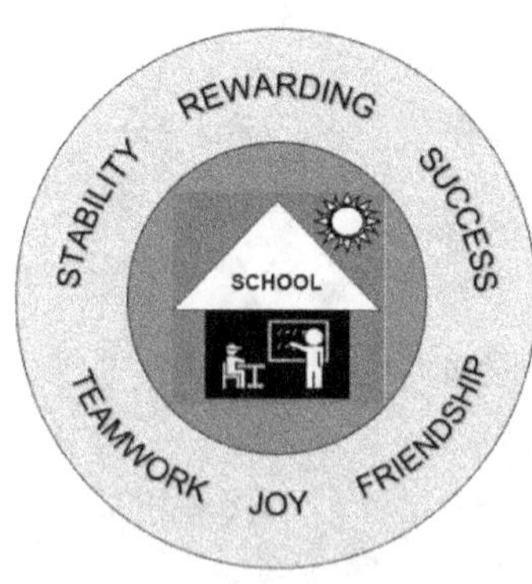

Or, is it, perhaps, good relationships with peers, classmates, or teammates? Whatever they are, with clear and solid values, we can transit smoothly this stage of life while developing our integrity.

However, let's not forget that, even when we have this new independency to a certain degree, we are still responsible to our parents during these formative years.

Values regarding the society

Social groups are next. This circle is very important because it is strongest during these years, when we are most vulnerable to be influenced by strangers.

We'll have friends and acquaintances, some in flesh and blood who we'll meet at parties, at gatherings, and at school. And some others who will be just virtual; those may be some of our "friends" on Instagram, Facebook, WhatsApp, computer games... That is, on the internet.

It is true that internet brings people "together." But it is also true that it brings all kinds of people, with blessings and also curses, and who can influence, one way or another, our values.

It seems normal to find these days teenagers who tend to listen more to their friends than to their parents. The issue is that some are not real friends. They are not.

"Anyone can claim to be your friend, but some
people are friends in name only."
Sirach 37:1 [a]

They will not care when we are in trouble and they will not help us when we are in need. They will not provide sincere advice and they will not visit us when we are sick. They may not be more mature than us, and will have, perhaps, different values and beliefs. Sadly, in many cases, they become "mentors" and, therefore, the main voices we listen to. And such "mentorship" can be happening without us leaving home, right in front of everybody's nose.

School is, indeed, a key stage of our life when values can be fortified or be twisted. Only with solid values and blessings, accumulated since our childhood, can we cope, confidently, with such an evil attack.

Values regarding the country

What about our country? In many developed countries, and some not so developed, people take for granted that their country will always be the way they know it, forever. But the devil is also after it, ready to take the smallest opportunity to strike and induce a country to flip upside down, filling it with curses. There are several examples in the world. Witness today the examples of Cuba, Venezuela, and Nicaragua, all on just one continent. The values we set for our country are worth fighting for. Don't rest on one's laurels. A country that falls victim to evil, will see its citizens fall too. Deceit, corruption, division, manipulation, injustice, repression, terrorism... All these elements will start cascading and eventually eroding the society, the families, and the individuals.

The question again:

'What do I value of my country?'

It could be its diverse nature or its natural resources. But also, it could be its people. Perhaps its welfare systems. Or maybe its safety. What are those for you?

Values regarding the planet

Last but not least, it's our planet. This surrounding circle that sometimes seems not many people care about since, anyway, someone else is taking care of it; so we like to think. Our planet is being hit very hard and, sadly, billions of people don't seem to realize it... or care. Global warming, scarcity of water, and pollution; for many, these are problems for future generations. So, why should we bother now? Well, those are our problems too, and they will be impacting us harder and harder, one way or another, and sooner rather than later. But, certainly, to the future generations, including the one of our own children and grandchildren. What kind of legacy will we be leaving them? Hopefully a good one.

Our contribution for a better world is to fight for our values... knowing, of course, what actually they are. Perhaps we value the four seasons that color our planet every year. Perhaps the air we breath and the water we drink.

In summary, values, both fundamental and pivot, will drive our thoughts, feelings, wishes, attitudes, and behaviour. And our values, being solid and strong, will shape our reality; the reality that we want to live for.

THIRD PRINCIPLE

DON'T LET PARADIGMS TWIST YOUR VALUES

It is only when we reach the age of reason that we start becoming conscious of our faculties; that is, we are now capable to understand that an event has a subject and an object, produces an effect that has a cause, and that such an event has occurred during a specific length of time and in a determined place. We become aware of our own acts and their consequences.

We also start developing our attentiveness; that is, to be able to concentrate our senses onto a specific event. And we start growing our capacity of observation, which is the applied or sustained attention to an event or our surroundings. Both the attention and observation open us up to a whole external and internal world, not very well understood until then; and through our own reflection, which is our internal analysis of what it is being observed.

Reflections

These reflections, in addition to the information received, give us the capacity to infer a judgment on others or on events, proceeding from one or several known truths to another truth that we cannot immediately perceive. This is judging. The issue here is that such judgments, and their "truths", remain stubbornly, sometimes forever, creating assumptions and paradigms that may ultimately impact our values.

Values drive our behaviour, as we said already. The information we receive during the critical years of our growth journey will contribute to the creation and consolidation of our values. However, information can also go the other way around and destroy or diminish our values. We process information when we perceive something one way, making us assume what the end result will be every time we perceive the same input. This develops later into becoming a paradigm that will be very difficult to change. Although not impossible.

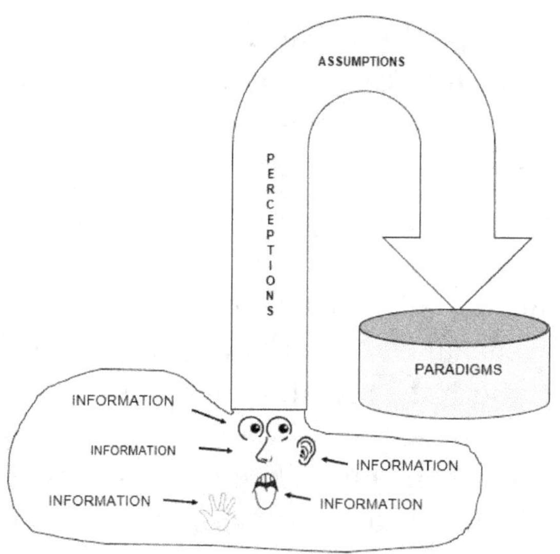

Perceptions and perspectives

To perceive is to become aware of situations through our senses: sight, smell, hearing, taste, and touch. Each person has one or two senses more developed than the others. Someone can perceive an atmosphere of relaxation by simply watching the running stream of water, while another by the sound of the water as it runs by.

Other definitions refer to the making of opinions based on appearances, that is, we develop our understanding on a fact, which it's based on how it appears before our senses. We perceive something by the way it is presented. It is here where the concept of perspective plays an important role. How we perceive something will depend on the perspective from which we are looking.

Probably the simplest way to explain perceptions and perspectives is when we look at something from afar as opposed to up close. That change of perspective moves the focus of what we see, making us appreciate, very likely, another element that is present, but we did not perceive it when we originally observed the object or situation.

For example, we could judge the bonsai shown on the left to be a piece of work that is masterfully and ingeniously crafted, giving us the perception of having been made by an expert who is extraordinarily patient and careful, industrious and diligent, meticulous, and with a solid knowledge on creating bonsais.

Now, getting closer, we may now see an element that we had missed and that suddenly enhances the work, making us, perhaps, feel more satisfied, bringing a smile to our face, and even modifying now our perception of the creator of the bonsai to be a detailed, caring and heart-warmed person.

Another good example is the Nazca lines, in Peru. These are a number of magnificent drawings on the ground, depicting several animals, insects, and shapes, which we can only see from a plane at high altitude. If we are on the ground, there is not much we can see, except a collection of rocks and perhaps a possible pathway, as shown on the picture below, on the right.

Monkey. Public Domain, https://commons. wikimedia.org/w/index.php?curid= 3037995

Nazca line from the ground. Trip Advisor.

Another simple example. Try looking at something at night compared to when you look at it during the day. We see it differently. Perspectives change our perceptions of things. In some cases so dramatically that what we see is just an illusion, like the pavement drawings of Julian Beever, the British drawing artist. He can, skilfully, draw something on a sidewalk, just a flat coloured drawing, which becomes a three-dimensional drawing when we look at it through a camera that he installs in front of the drawings.

People may also try to change perceptions by "justifying" the situation: 'I stole some money because I was hungry;' 'I lied to you, so you were not hurt;' 'I cheated on you because I suspected you were cheating on me.' In all cases, justifying our actions by practically blaming others, or something else, will just add to our curses, and that will only bring misery.

Assumptions

During our life, we are continuously perceiving things, making us compile assumptions; all based on the information we have gathered along the way. And when we assume something, we believe that things are the way they are or that something will happen in a certain way without having any proof.

For example, on a cloudy day, the trees are moving vigorously, making us perceive through our eyes and skin the surrounding darkness and the strong wind, and immediately we assume it is going to rain. On a bright day, we look through the window and see people walking outside, dressed in T-shirts and shorts, carrying a bottle of water, making us assume it is a very hot day. Or perhaps we are listening to loud music coming from our neighbour's flat, and we assume he is having a party for his friends, as he has done before.

From these examples, once we were aware of the situation, we "knew" what was happening or about to happen. The question here is: are we, then, assuming that it will be like that all the time?

We are always assuming. We assume that, by covering our heads from the rain, we will not get sick; we assume our children will do well at school because we hire private tutors; we assume we'll get a pay rise this year because we had one last year. Certainly, we take many assumptions for granted. How disappointing would it be if what really happens is not what we had assumed?

So, if our assumption is, or will be, of a significant impact, we better do something about it. That is, either make it happen, or prevent it from happening, depending on which way we want the result pan out. Otherwise, the result can become an unexpected shock for us.

We can assume we will be healthy for the next 20 years, if we take good care of ourselves. We can assume we may not get sick, if we are conscious enough to not stay too long in the rain or, perhaps, taking some extra vitamin C; or having a flu shot. We may assume our children will do well, but we could check their homework regularly. We could assume we'll get still a pay rise this year if we are industrious and responsible, but perhaps we should also be prudent and not incur in any extra unnecessary expenditures in case we don't get the pay rise.

This behaviour could only occur if we have strong values and if we have grown in blessings. Without them, we could be careless, irresponsible, and lazy, and then end up becoming sick or overwhelmed in debt.

Generalizations

The more our assumptions are proven correct, the easier it is to generalize. Generalization is to form a judgment in which we implicitly apply a set of characteristics, properties, and outcomes to a whole group, class, type, genre, breed, generation, situation, and so on, all of which we saw repeated on some individual cases. This is dangerous and can add curses, if we don't know how to control it.

For example, we may read about a couple of cases involving lawyers who were found guilty of taking millions of dollars from their clients; or a priest in one country, and another one in a different country, who were both found guilty of child abuse. Because one or two individuals behave wrongly, some may think all lawyers and all priests are the same. Even larger groups can't escape from unfair judgment. We may read that a particular ethnic race is involved in the majority of crimes in the city. That will probably make us heighten our safety awareness when we see a member of that race approaching us. We could be judging incorrectly because of generalization.

What may happen, then, if we don't grow our blessings? Well, we start distorting our values. For example, we may question our faith 'because "all" priests abuse youngsters.' Or we may question marriage and family 'because my parents and many of my friends have divorced.' Even the value of friendship and acceptance may be compromised 'because this boy is of that troublesome ethnic race.' How terrible! That will only bring curses like rejection, mistrust, resentment, criticism, and even hatred.

Adults can make a conscious judgment of the situation, and not let these assumptions twist their values. But, what about our youngsters, whose values and blessings are still under development? Therefore, the sooner we grow blessings, the better... Before assumptions become paradigms.

Paradigms

We all have many paradigms. Paradigms are strong beliefs in a model or a pattern, and can be personal as well as cultural. Many can affect our daily life, in different degrees. "Cereals are only for breakfast;" "porridge is for toddlers;" "mother's milk is only for babies;" "only those who excel in math and physics can be good engineers;" "insects are not food for humans." For sure, there will be sufficient reasons that support many of these paradigms, especially when the underlying assumptions are repeatedly proven correct.

Paradigms, however, are continuously challenged, especially in these modern times, and youngsters have an advantage as they are much more likely to question everything. Like that one who asked: 'Why does the round pizza come in a square box but we eat it in triangles?'

Paradigm shift

When we accumulate new information and knowledge as we grow, we may start challenging our own paradigms, and then an opportunity opens up for us to change them and possibly learn something. So, we may discover later in life that there is more than one religion in the world; that cars can be driven either on the right or on the left; and that other people live according to a different calendar: while we live in the year 2019, others live in year 1440 (Islamic calendar) or year 2562 (Buddhist calendar)!

When the usual and accepted way of doing or thinking

about something is changed, a paradigm shift occurs. The Concise Oxford Dictionary defines paradigm shift as "a fundamental change in approach of the underlying assumption." But challenging paradigms is a way to think deeper and ultimately solidify your thoughts, feelings, wishes, attitudes and behaviours, although on many occasions that doesn't come without a fight. The whole world sometimes is in a mood to change many old paradigms, which, for some, could be disappointing, but not for others, as in providing the same washroom for both male and female and not a separate one, like when our parents or even ourselves grew up.

We are seeing greater changes in the world. A few decades ago, in several societies, spanking children was assumed to be the best practice to make them behave properly. Also, it was unthinkable to consider a legal conjugal union of two people of the same sex, and people were either strictly male or female. Ice-creams were sold in no flavours other than chocolate, vanilla, or strawberry. E-sports, non-existent then, are now filling stadiums with spectators; while some doctors are even talking nowadays of head transplants. These and many other changes are making us ponder whether to accept or not that the world is changing, for the better or for the worse, and that many of the old beliefs have now become obsolete.

Well, indeed, the world is changing, and will continue doing so for the worse if our values are warped. Of course, the more we learn and our knowledge expands, our minds start questioning everything. We try to do, and accept, bolder things, without realizing that in many of the proposed changes it is the devil himself and his minions who are behind it all, whispering in our ears telling us that it is fine to accept the changes that come along, because "it is a new world out there." We hear that everything can be "improved" and there are better ways to accomplish anything; and that change is the only constant. From the outside, some changes may look safe, subtle, justified, and needed, and, consequently, the old paradigms are replaced by new ones. We better stay vigilant.

Go forth, only if our values are strengthened

But our growth journey is still ours and how we want our thoughts, feelings, wishes, attitudes, and behaviours to be is also ours; not someone else's. When the "world" presents us with changes or new ways to go, perhaps we should take a deeper look at them to find out if the outcome is going to be a blessing or a curse; if it is for or against our values. Not because everyone else is changing, do we have to also change... Unless it is for strengthening our values and for growing our blessings. Our values must remain firm and solid, and no paradigm, shifted or not, should break them.

FOURTH PRINCIPLE

GET ADVICE

"The devil is wiser for being old rather than for being devil."

This is a popular saying in several of the Latin-American countries. It could be true, considering that the devil has been around for a long, long time.

"The voice of the experience," another statement we hear quite a lot when an expert talks. Not questionable, people are born, they grow, and they live. Knowledge, gained through both education and instruction, in addition of one's own experiences, are accumulated continuously. Indeed, wisdom requires lots of time to be replete with knowledge and experiences; that wisdom will then allow us, when facing new situations, to assume, to analyse, to make decisions, and to eventually learn from the outcome. Certainly, we learn from our successes as well as from our mistakes. Why, then, do we prove, over and over again, that man is the only "animal" that makes the same mistake twice? Well, "to err is human," they say.

Are we simply justifying with that adage the fact that we can repeat a mistake? Do we keep on trying because we don't accept failure and we will repeat it again and again until we get it right, knowing that repeating something, we increase the probability that the desired outcome will eventually happen? Or is it because we don't learn fast enough? Or maybe because we are just stubborn?

Actually, we do learn something, always. After doing something once or ten times, we do learn. It is not that man does not learn fast... well, maybe some faster than others; but we learn because we have our brain and our five senses. We perceive things, we assume, and we'll try to prove that our assumptions are right. It is true that learning from personal experience is more powerful than learning from other people's experience, but we should never underestimate the knowledge accumulated by others, especially those who have lived longer than us. To accept that, we need to be blessed with humbleness. We need to be humble enough to accept that we don't know everything, that we can learn from others who have learnt, lived, and experienced more than us. Why not then ask for their advice? Don't let pride, a curse, overcome you.

Education versus Instruction

Education and instruction are sometimes taken as being identical, as fully interchangeable. For example, many employment application forms ask for the "education" history of the candidates, and the candidates will usually fill it in with information related to the subjects in which they were instructed (accounting, engineering, librarian, carpentry, etc.) and naming the institution where they received their diploma. And that is acceptable to the employer, because that is what he anyway wanted in the first place.

When we are being educated, we are perfecting all our faculties, both moral and intellectual... And we could also include our physical achievements as well. The objective of education is to make us think, feel, wish, and act wisely and rightfully. The more educated we are, the more blessings we'll have, and the more rewarding and enjoyable our growth journey will be.

When we are being instructed, we are accumulating knowledge. We are also developing our intelligence, talents, and skills.

> "Anything you say to the wise, will make them
> wiser. Whatever you tell the righteous will add to
> their knowledge."
> *Proverbs 9:9* [a]

We gain instruction through ideas, facts, information, and knowledge transfer. Knowledge is, indeed, powerful and it can be a very profitable personal value. Take the example of the factory manager who couldn't start a machine and, feeling helpless, brought in an expert from outside to help fix it. The expert came, saw, pressed a button, and the machine started. Everybody was happy until the invoice came for $1,000. Appalled, the factory manager asked the expert why his charges were $1,000, when the only thing he did was to press a button. He then requested a detailed invoice. And the detailed invoice came: $1 for pressing a button and $999 for knowing which button to press.

Instruction is indeed an important element that complements a strong education. They complement each other. A NASA scientist could be, without education, a real uncouth individual, piling up curses and becoming arrogant, contemptuous, proud, banal, pretentious, and insolent. On the other hand, a humble, honest, and religious preacher may not have enough skills, learnings, and knowledge to teach God's message to others.

Many blessings come from the holistic accumulation of education, as in being just and fair, creative, assertive, efficient, professional, and rewarding, to name just a few. But probably the most valuable lesson of education is the lesson of morality, providing us with the capacity of discerning between what is right and what is wrong. We could be very well instructed in the handling of a gun, but are we going to use it?

Education and instruction begin even before we have awareness of own being. At home, we will be educated to be faithful, to be responsible, to be respectful. Our parents teach us obedience, discipline, good manners, and also how to eat our meals and to speak our language. At that young age, we don't realize that our parent's advice comes entirely out of love, sincerity, and good wishes, and that it will never be ill-intentioned. But the seed has been sown and it will bear fruit a few years later.

Logically, at that early age, our surrounding circles are few and small. However, as these circles grow, instruction becomes more predominant for us. We leave home to start compiling information from teachers, tutors, and experts. All kinds of information. Hopefully, by then, we should have absorbed solid values and have accumulated many blessings, enough to protect us against the curses that swarm the world.

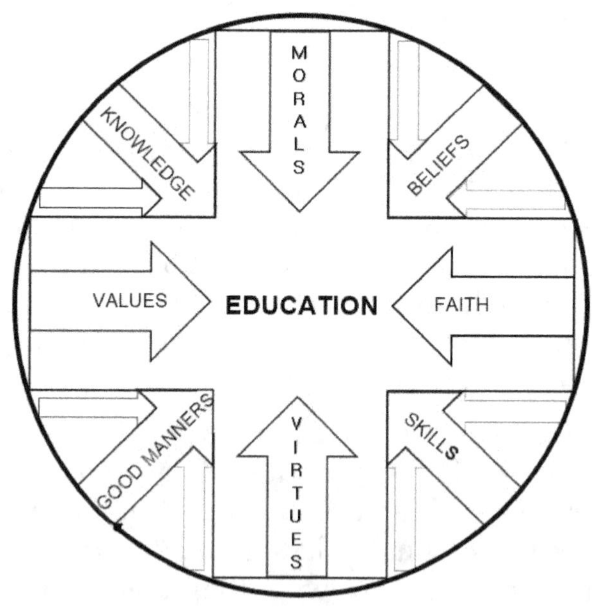

By the end of childhood and adolescence, even after entering into the adult age, we have accumulated and digested piles and piles of information. At school, we'll be instructed in different subjects, like science, accounting, chemistry or literature. We will also start listening to our peers, more than we'll listen to our parents; and not only listening, but also believing. Later, at the work place, we will reinforce some more values to guide us on future objectives that we wish to pursue.

But, how much of that teaching from teachers and peers went to our education and how much went to our instruction? The answer is not that important, as long as all of that contributes to our integrity. And how much is enough? Well, many still think that with whatever knowledge they have amassed, they know everything.

> "Never let yourself think that you are wiser than
> you are."
> *Proverbs 3:7* [a]

Being pompous is one thing, but being naive is another. The reality is that we don't know everything. That we'll always need more knowledge and education. And we can always ask those who know and have lived longer than us.

Get advice, get far

Getting advice is a wise thing to do, enabling us to move forward and solve problems; or recover from poor situations that we may encounter on our growth journey.

> "If you listen to advice and are willing to learn,
> one day you will be wise."
> *Proverbs 19:20* [a]

At school, when we don't know an answer in chemistry, we ask the chemistry teacher (not the literature teacher!). We simply go to the best source of advice. Some of our teachers may become tutors and some of our friends with more experience can become our mentors. Their experiences can teach us something, so, at least, we don't start from zero. We can learn from their successes, as well as from their mistakes.

> "Gold and silver provide security, but good advice
> is better."
> *Sirach 40:25* [a]

We don't have all what it takes to face each and every situation that we will encounter in life. Moreover, we may approach a situation "boxed in" by our limited tools: skills, knowledge, and experience that we possess, which may not be enough. But other people may have gone through a similar situation, and they can help us prevent making mistakes, so we can continue to move forward.

> "Find someone who is wise, and stay with him."
> *Sirach 6:34* [a]

Why then, sometimes, are we so reluctant to seek advice from others? If we don't listen to advice, we'll make the same mistakes that others have made... only adding to our sorrows, knowing that they could have been prevented.

> "If you refuse good advice, you are asking for
> trouble; follow it and you are safe."
> *Proverbs 13:13* [a]

There is another popular saying in some Latin-American countries: "The one who doesn't hear advice will not reach old age." In most cases, advice is a free resource and readily available from our parents, tutors, mentors, and people with more experience. We just have to open up ourselves to get advice, not to get defensive, and sit down to ask and then listen. Let's remember what Jesus said:

> "Ask, and you will receive; seek, and you will find;
> knock, and the door will be opened to you."
> *Matthew 7:7* [a]

If we don't hear advice, we'll make unnecessary mistakes, and making mistakes will only stop us or, the very least, delay us in our growth journey. We won't get very far by repeating mistakes.

> "Apply your heart to instruction, and your ears to
> words of wisdom."
> *Proverbs 23:12* [b]

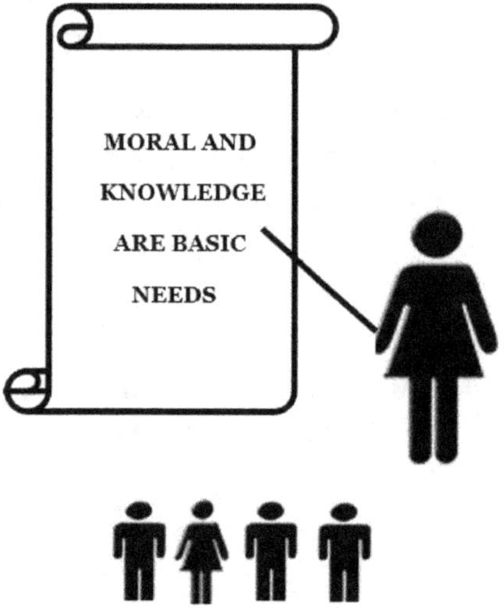
MORAL AND
KNOWLEDGE
ARE BASIC
NEEDS

FIFTH PRINCIPLE

BETTER SAFE THAN SORRY

Every mistake we make and every failure we go through in life will only add to our tribulations, adding weight to our crosses. Henceforth, we should strive for fewer mistakes; the fewer mistakes we make, the less chance of failure.

A mistake is an action, decision, or judgment that produces an unwanted result. This unwanted result is, of course, unintentional. But, looking at it positively, that is something that we can still learn from, placing us in a better position should this situation happen again. So, we should not necessarily conclude that we "failed" by making a mistake. A failure is the lack of success in a more holistic way. Failing gives us little chance to turn things around. We failed and we failed; so, likely, no more chances. But dealing with mistakes is not the same as dealing with failures, and the pain that we suffer from each are also different. We can lose many battles, meaning we can make many mistakes, but with the right attitude, determination, courage, and preventive approach, we can still succeed in whatever we are doing. We can still win the war.

We learnt in the last chapter that many mistakes can be avoided by listening to the well-intentioned advice from our parents and from those with more experience and knowledge than ourselves. But many mistakes can also be avoided, if we think in advance about what can go wrong and do something about it. That is prevention.

Prevention

Prevention is defined as stopping something from happening or someone from doing something. But let's be clear on the real concept; we do not want to prevent something *good* from happening. This would be obstruction, avoidance, or deterring. Imagine we prevent someone from helping a neighbour in need; that would only count as a curse. What we want to prevent is something *bad* from occurring. We want to prevent curses by working on our blessings. And one blessing that supports prevention is prudence. In this context, prevention is a blessing.

> "The prudent man is cautious in everything; when
> sin abounds, he will keep away from wrongdoing".
> *Sirach 18:27* [b]

Logically, we don't want a *problem* to happen. We want to prevent it, simply because it is better to avoid it rather than to deal with it after it has happened. That is why we hear sayings like: "Prevention is better than cure," "An ounce of prevention is worth a pound of cure," "Better safe than sorry."

And so on. These are very wise sayings, indeed. Prevention can save us from mistakes and failures... and tribulations.

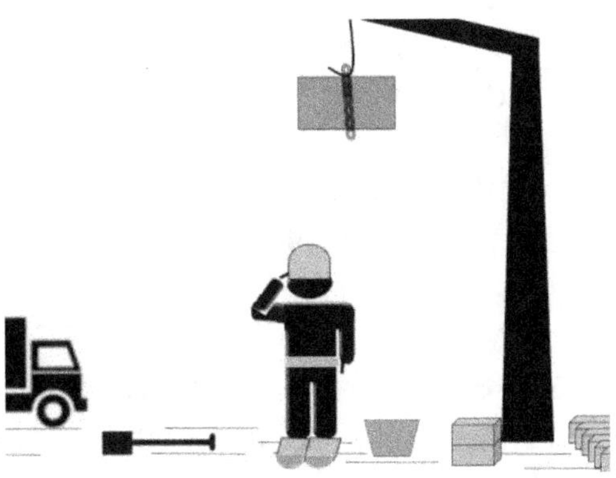

Prevention is a blessing that doesn't come to us so easily. We tend to take whatever assumptions we have for granted. It may not occur to us, spontaneously, that something different may happen, so we don't act in advance upon other possible outcomes, or likely consequences. And because of that, we wouldn't consider any other result or if such possible outcomes could happen. A strong wind and dark skies would make us assume it is going to rain. Why then wait until it is actually raining, before taking the umbrella? We cannot stop the rain by just taking the umbrella, but we can prevent ourselves from getting wet and, possibly, getting sick. Or perhaps we could avoid being late to school, by foreseeing the heavy traffic that usually builds up when it rains; or the difficulty in getting a cab.

Happily, preventing bad situations from happening could be easy and straight forward in many cases. Avoid arriving late at school by leaving home early; prevent an illness by getting a vaccination or keeping your body healthy; avoid getting hurt when using a machine by getting the right training, or by using the right tool; prevent bankruptcy by getting an insurance or by saving money; prevent a miserable old age by doing exercise and eating well; prevent losses by fire by keeping a fire extinguisher and not storing inflammable materials; prevent floods in town by building drainage canals; and so on.

"Sensible people are careful to stay out of trouble;
but stupid people are careless and act too quickly."
Proverbs 14:16 [a]

We can prevent bad events from happening at each circle that surround us. Yes, it could be overwhelming to start seeing potential hazards and dangers everywhere, and the idea is not to become paranoiac about it; but by protecting what we value, as a conscious effort, will make us think that way and, henceforth, we will end up applying prevention naturally into future situations.

Clear goals and objectives

To implement prevention, we first need to know what goals and objectives we want to achieve, both short and long term. Growing our values, both fundamental and pivot, and accumulating blessings should be some of our goals in life, and they need to be executed assuredly and expeditiously. So, this could be a good way to start. But of course, there are other minor goals that could be helped significantly by applying some prevention, like a school science project that we need to finish by tomorrow, a company sales target that we need to hit by the end of the month, or reducing an extra 5 kgs from our bodyweight.

Next, it is to know the process required to get to that target, objective, or to the final goal. We need to know the best and the second-best route or way to get there, and what obstacles we may find along the way; what can go wrong or go against us. We need to watch and study the surroundings, the environment in which such situations will evolve. We need to identify the factors that will contribute for an expeditious and successful result.

We certainly need to do the due diligence on everything related to the goal we have set in mind to achieve: investigate, get advice, read about it. The science project will not be finished, if we don't allow enough time or with the necessary studying; or without the required materials. Our sales target will not be hit if we don't know our competitors, our customers and their constraints, needs and motivations. And we will not reduce our weight, if we keep indulging ourselves with sweets.

Finally, make a plan. Define what to do, when to do it, how to do it, with whom, where, and with what resources. And then, just get to it, act on it!

> "After all, you must make careful plans before you
> fight the battle, and the more good advice you get,
> the more likely you are to win."
> *Proverbs 24:6* [a]

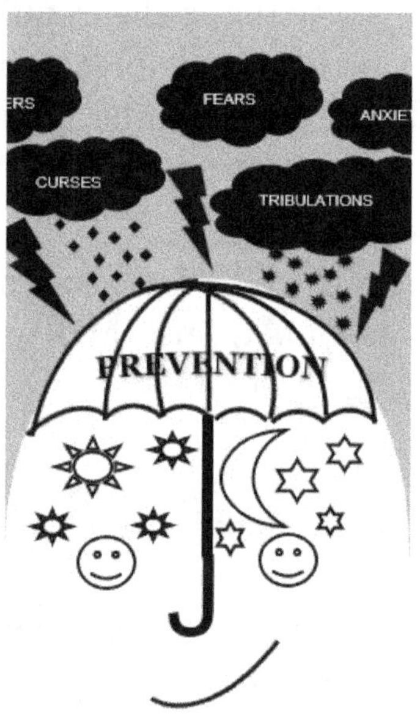
ERS
FEARS
ANXIET
CURSES
TRIBULATIONS
PREVENTION

SIXTH PRINCIPLE

COMPARE TO THE BEST

'Wait a minute!' We have been told, many times by the gurus of personal growth, not to compare ourselves to anyone else; that we are individuals with our own set of beliefs, feelings, struggles, wishes, rationale, and decision-making prowess. 'We will not compare ourselves to others!'

Well, it is true. When we compare ourselves to others, without the necessary maturity and solid blessings, we may fall into curses. We may feel envy, pity, conformism, pride, arrogance, and superiority -or feelings of inferiority. And if we fall into those curses, we could become stuck and paralyzed. This is not what we want, of course. The comparison to make is not based on our own inner core as human beings, but should be based on our actions and behaviours. Simply because we can always behave better. Since comparisons are more likely to be made on results, we just need to keep in mind that results are the consequence of our behaviour. So, what we need to compare are our actions and behaviours to reach a righteous and positive result.

Comparison is a daily affair

Life is not a contest... Or is it? Well, we compete with others in many situations in life, whether we like it or not, and if there is competition, then there is comparison. And there are all kinds of competition, at all levels. The job vacancy goes to the person considered to be better than the rest for such position. The trophy goes to the team that performed best of all. To participate in the Olympics, or even at the local games, we need to qualify in our particular sporting discipline. Not everyone can aspire to be a professor at Harvard University, let alone to be awarded a Nobel prize. So, whether we compare ourselves consciously to others, or it is someone who is comparing us to someone else, we are objects of comparison. No escape; we live in a competitive world. Even governments of some countries encourage competition, so their society evolves better by pushing its individuals to achieve the very best out of themselves.

Even if we are reluctant to be subjects of any comparison, there may be instances where we may feel satisfaction when someone compare us... depending on to whom we are being compared! If we play soccer and someone says we play like Cristiano Ronaldo, we feel good, don't we? But probably we wouldn't feel as good if someone accuses us of thinking like Hitler. In other words, many will not reject comparison, if the comparison is against the best.

Instinct of survival

In many instances, we are not conscious that we are also making comparisons. When we need advice, we will choose from among the experts who can give us the best advice. We will stick to the handyman with whom we were more satisfied, after trying a couple. We may choose one restaurant over another because of the chef. It is really a competitive world out there. Even gambling in a lottery, when we know it is all about probability, we may end up buying more than one ticket, hoping to beat the others and win the first prize. It is the instinct of survival; the Darwin's Law.

Life is not a contest and yet, we can all win

Everything we do should not really become a contest or competition. It will only add tribulations to ourselves, making our cross heavier. But if we are not reaching our goals, consistently and efficiently, it is because we are doing something wrong. However, other people appear to be doing things right.

We have to acknowledge that there are people out there who are really good; achieving wonderful things. We see them as winners. We indeed must appreciate the success of others and the effort they make to reach their goals, and to honestly rejoice in ourselves for their success. That's a blessing.

So, if other people succeed, it is because they are good, if not the best, in whatever discipline they are working to reach their goals. And their goals may the same, or similar, to those that we pursue. Therefore, wouldn't be logical to learn what they did, when they did it, and how they did it, so that we may also succeed in achieving our goals? We can indeed compare what we are doing with what the most successful people are doing so we can all, then, be winners too!

Yes, there may be people who really don't care about how others are doing, or whether there are better ways to do something; some people indeed don't care how to get better results. Well, these people are not after self-improvement; they are conformist. They won't learn and they won't get too far. Their actions and behaviours are both vulnerable to being driven by curses. This assertion could be an extreme, certainly, but the point being made here is that we need to reflect on whether we are being passive and indifferent.

Our heroes

When we are children, we see our father and our mother as the best people in the entire world. They are our heroes; we admire them and we follow them. They are simply the best. We see how they do things, their moves, their behaviour; and we learn from them. Later, understandably, some other leaders and heroes will also appear; the very best in a wide variety of endeavours. Certainly, better than us.

How can I be part of the London Symphony Orchestra? Or play for Real Madrid? Or study at the National University of Singapore? If we want to achieve these aspirations, but we are not yet there, we could ask ourselves a few questions:

- 'What are my shortfalls compared to the best?'
- 'What am I lacking that the best in the field have?'
- 'What am I doing differently from the best?'
- 'What else can I do to improve?'

There are many things that we can learn from the best: assertive approaches, useful techniques, required skills, thorough knowledge, necessary resources, hands-on training, relevant contacts, effective measurements and indicators, etc. And not only technical matters. There are people who stand out in blessings, in a way much better than we do. They are more helpful, sympathetic, organized, respectful, neat, and merciful, to mention just a few. What do they do that we don't?

But let's be mindful. If we feel envy or resentment when we see the success of others, we are not ready. If we rejoice or feel proud because we did better than others, we are not ready. And if we are not ready, we should continue working on our blessings, such as humility, humbleness, respect, acceptance. Keep growing on your blessings, so as not to delay your growth journey.

Compare yourself to the best. Never compare yourself to the worst for consolation. If we didn't do well in an exam, are we going to console ourselves by being compared to the one who failed? Are we going to feel happier because we were not the lowest on the sales chart? Are we going to compare ourselves to the person who look to the other side, ignoring someone in need of help, so we feel "relieved" because we would do the same? Compare yourself to the best.

FINISH

SEVENTH PRINCIPLE

FOCUS ON THE GOAL

So, now we know what we want to reach for, and where to go; also, the obstacles that may arise, and some ways to prevent them from becoming roadblocks that are hard to move; plus, a pretty good idea how the experts would do it. Are we all set to reach our goals?

On many occasions, voluntarily or not, we lose track of our priorities. We may get distracted. For example, a high level of instruction could be one of our values, so getting a university diploma or certificate should be a priority. But, instead of focusing on getting such a diploma, we allow computer games, girlfriends or boyfriends, parties, adventures, and other interests to interfere and distract us from our priorities.

It is indeed quite easy to get distracted. Of course, we need to do other things; to do different activities and to pursue different interests. And that's alright, as long as they also bring us blessings and are driven by our values; otherwise, we are going in the wrong direction and wasting our time and our life.

Vision

To focus on a goal, it first requires us to see ourselves

achieving that goal. We have to visualize it, without thinking just yet, of the time and other resources it would take; just visualize it. If you don't see yourself having kids, you may never have them. We will never be a pilot, a singer, or a preacher, if we never imagine it first. We first visualize something. Everything starts with an idea, a vision, or a thought, and reality comes later. Jules Verne (1828-1905) talked about going to the moon (book 'From the Earth to the Moon,' 1865) or going around the world (book 'Around the World in 80 days,' 1873), at a time when these notions were pure science-fiction. It was only in May 1927 when Charles Lindbergh could fly his airplane *The Spirit of St Louis* across the Atlantic, which was the world's first transatlantic flight. The TV series of 'The Jetsons,' aired during the 1960's, already showed telephone calls with video; this only became a commercial reality decades later! We really have to visualize ourselves doing or achieving something, in order to make it happen. But how many times have we said to a proposition, "I don't see myself doing that," "I just can't," or something like that? And these are statements that only add weight to our crosses.

The concept of having a vision is not new at all. Corporations and institutions have had them for many years as part of their philosophy and culture. They need to see where they want to be in 5- or 10-years' time. That is the focus, the direction, the goal to aim for.

Every project, whether it is for development or for improvement, requires a plan, even for the simplest things. Just going to the movies needs a plan. We plan what movie, where and when to watch it, and how to get to the cinema; and maybe, also, with whom. We may do this unconsciously, but that is still a plan. However, many other goals are more complex, and when there is a complex goal, one of the main issues at hand is whether the goal may disappear over the horizon; either because there are too many steps and actions to complete, or simply because we become discouraged.

We should never deviate our eyes from the goal. Try to draw a straight line between two dots on a paper, say 50cm apart. Start drawing from the first dot towards the second, but without looking at that second dot; just try and see how "straight" that line will be.

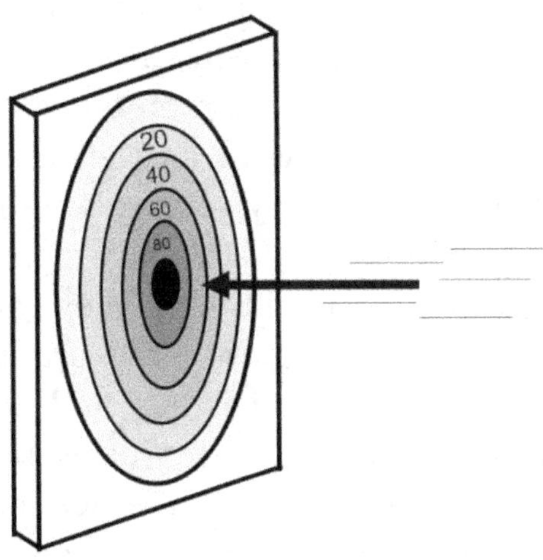

Set objectives

If a goal is too complex, then we had better set intermediate objectives, but with our ultimate goal always in mind. By setting intermediate objectives, we will not feel overwhelmed and breathless, which may, consequently, discourage us from continuing. It is like climbing a long staircase; by looking directly at each step we take, or just to the next split landing, we'll easily get to the top. If we are 10kg overweight, perhaps 1 kg per week during a 10-week trial, may sound a reasonable reduction target. If we want to bring back to the family our stranded brother, or a friend, calling him on the phone this week, to learn how he is, could be a good way to start. To prohibit the use of plastic straws at the food court, or of plastic bags at the shop, could make a small contribution to reduce pollution on our planet. Small objectives, and we can go far; just make sure that they are all towards our goals.

Certainly, setting and achieving objectives will make us move forward and make us feel that we are not standing still or stuck in life. Should we fall down in this effort, we may find ourselves lost, and that will give curses a chance to appear, and tribulations to pile up on our crosses. But these objectives should be meaningful as well as challenging; in other words, they should really require an effort from us. If we set up an objective of say a 250g weight reduction per week, we may likely feel we will not achieve anything. As the saying goes, "no pain, no gain". We are not gaining in courage, endurance, and stoicism... and neither are we reducing our weight! Of course, by just setting challenging objectives, it does not necessarily guarantee that we will move forward, unless there is commitment to achieve them. For so many, their New Year's resolutions remain just that... resolutions. We must fully commit to do what it takes to reach out objectives, until we achieve the final goal.

Set targets

When setting our objectives, we need to define the associated targets, which are basically short-term objectives or actions, or commitments. We may decide not to eat any sweets in the next four weeks, or we may decide to call our brother once this week and again in three weeks' time. We may run for 30 minutes at a time, three days a week; or smile to a stranger every day. These targets set us in the right direction to achieve our goal of being healthy; or having a harmonious family or social life.

Value-added actions

We must always pay attention to whether our targets or actions are really effective, relevant, and to the point; in other words, "value added". An action is of no value if it contradicts another objective, let alone going against a life's goal. You shouldn't buy a treadmill machine to help you reduce your weight, if that's going to affect your finances, which in turn may unsettle your peace of mind; or even worse.

On the contrary, an action or target will be of more value if it also leverages support to your other objectives and goals. If we value, for example, both a high level of instruction and wealth, then targeting to complete a diploma that includes learning another language may help.

To achieve whatever target, objective, or goal we set, we need to cultivate and develop blessings, like perseverance, resilience, and determination. Everything that is driven by our values is always worthwhile to pursue. It will be what makes us grow, accumulate blessings, reduce curses, and thus carry a lighter cross throughout our life journey.

> "An intelligent person aims at a wise action, but a
> fool starts off in many directions."
> *Proverbs 17:24* [a]

EIGHTH PRINCIPLE

GET TO IT... ACT NOW!

"No one moves without taking a first step."

We can always think of thousands of excuses, obstacles on the way, and of other priorities, so as not to do what we have to do. Even when we are completely prepared and consciously ready to go, we may start having second thoughts, hearing voices in our head saying that we will fail, or perhaps that it is not worth it; or that we are not truly prepared. Well, those voices don't come from God and we shouldn't entertain those thoughts.

Everything has a right time, true; but it is always sooner rather than later. As the saying says: "Don't leave for tomorrow what you can do today." And many times, we don't do what we have to do with the excuse that we are "patient"; we confuse patience with procrastination.

Don't procrastinate

The man who procrastinates will not act, even when being totally ready to act. Procrastinating has many consequences that will add to our tribulations. We may lose precious time; our self-esteem can diminish; our goals may be delayed; and frustration can take over.

We could still doubt of our readiness, especially if it is the very first time we try to do something. There are certainly cases when we don't really know whether we are ready or not. To help assess if we are ready enough to start something, we could just ask ourselves a couple of simple questions:

'Do I need more information, knowledge, resources, or advice?'

'Are the reasons to wait longer – or not– just clumsy or silly excuses?'

Procrastination will definitely take away from us the most precious resource we have: our time. And time is life. The problem that most people have is taking for granted that they'll always have plenty of time, making them think they can do everything later on. Indeed, we all think we will have many days ahead of us; all of 24 hours each. But assuming we do, aren't we anyway realizing that time lost is indeed really lost, that cannot ever be recovered, and that we cannot just take, buy, or borrow one second more?

Still, some will procrastinate in doing many things that may lead them to a life full of blessings, to rather do things that are not worth doing; and without realizing that their bodies continue to wear out and their energy is depleting. In other words, their life continually degenerating.

The reality is that no one knows how much time we have left. But whatever it is, it is short. Indeed, it is going to feel so short that many will end up asking themselves, 'What did I do with my time?', and the answer may not be a satisfactory one.

Don't waste time

Wasting time is a curse, and when people realize it and see the short time they have now left, they will panic. This, alarmingly, may bring others curses on them. Haven't we encountered people in the hurry out there, who become aggressive and rude, running over and insulting others, and being impatient, sneaky, or disruptive?

So, let's not waste time and get to it, act now! Let's put ourselves to work and gain blessings, avoid curses, and grow in our values. Will we encounter problems and issues during our growth journey? Yes, of course. For most advice, planning, knowledge and resources we have, there is always the possibility that something new arises, something that we, or anyone else for that matter, has never encountered before. Notwithstanding, this drawback we can still face it.

Face the obstacles

There is plenty of information out there about problem solving techniques that are well structured and detailed, aiming to increase the chance of a successful outcome. It is really important to tackle every problem and to address any obstacle or set back that shows up when we do commit to do something. We should never let a problem or issue stop us or discourage us.

There are several techniques to solve problems, but a very common approach is as follows:

- Identify the problem and describe it well.

- Find out possible root causes and list them in order of probability of being the real causes.

- Identify the best solution(s) for the root cause(s) and put it (them) into practice; a temporary solution may be needed in the meantime.

- Evaluate if the problem still persists; if so, review the root causes and their solutions.

- Implement preventive actions to avoid the root causes repeating themselves.

Of course, each step requires much more depth than described above. For example, to select the solution to be implemented, our decision will require considering the ease of implementation, the time it will take, the resources that will be needed, and the cost involved in implementing it. The solution must be effective. Letting ourselves be carried away only by the ease in implementing it or by its low cost, can make us incur in mistakes that will possibly result in failure or, at least, in wasting precious time and money.

Act now!

So, let's get to it and start doing what we have to do to reach our goals, as per our plan, and with determination and diligence. Be it reducing weight; be it bringing back the stranded brother; be it getting a high level of instruction; or be it becoming a kinder person.

Faith

But, above having absorbed all the knowledge and advice that the experts and the people who love us could give; above having foreseen all the obstacles and having implemented preventive actions to avoid them; and above having mastered problem-solving techniques to tackle any unforeseen problem, there is one blessing that will help us achieve our goals. One blessing that will cover everything and no matter if there is fragility, weakness, inconsistency, a crack, or divergence in the approach or in the process.... We will still succeed. This is faith. Our faith, even if it is the size of a mustard seed, can move mountains.

> "To have faith is to be sure of the things we hoped for; to be certain of the things we cannot see."
>
> *Hebrews 11:1 [a]*

NINTH PRINCIPLE

WHATEVER YOU DO, MAKE POSITIVE IMPACT ON OTHERS

To make someone feel loved is probably one of the most significant impacts we can make. Jesus said to love even our enemies. It is the second commandment. And that would require a lot of blessings. But there are also many other ways in which we make a significant and a positive impact on others, be them strangers or not.

There is no fruitful life if we don't make a positive impact on others. When we make a positive impact on someone, the satisfaction and reward are immeasurable, even if we don't realize it immediately. And the effort required is, in many cases, negligible. It is that easy.

Give

There is no such thing as "I don't need anything." There is always something that someone needs, wants, or wishes for. We may not need any material thing, but life is not only about materialism. We may need to laugh at some point; or talk to someone; or feel at peace. And if we are able to satisfy that need for someone, we are already creating a positive impact.

To create a positive impact, we have to give. Sitting

comfortably on a bench looking at the horizon will not provide much of an impact on others. We must give, and it is not necessarily materials things as already said. We have other things that are very precious, even more so than material things as, for example, our time. Time is limited; it is being consumed continuously, regardless of whether we use it or not, and it is non-renewable. But it is so precious that we should give it wisely, because we also need it for our own personal growth. Yet, a good portion of it can still be given to others, creating an opportunity to make a positive impact; even if it is merely companionship. Have you ever wished, while eating alone at the food court, that someone would be there with you? The feeling being sometimes so powerful that you hope that even a stranger sits at your table? But the impact will be even more significant if we accompany it with blessings. So, it is not only companionship we can give to someone, we can also give our love, generosity, kindness, compassion, care, respect, forgiveness, attention, and friendship... and more. And if the other person takes in even a portion of them, there is already a positive impact made.

Fighting a complex world

The world is now much more complex than before. We are not in the 1960's anymore, when everybody was professing peace and love in a world where many postmen were needed to deliver mail. This complexity makes our current world more unfamiliar, all of which makes us more careful, cautious, suspicious, and hesitant to give something to others, including our time. Of course, to give is easy between spouses, brothers and sisters, parents and children, uncles and nephews, cousins, friends, and those who are close to us. But...

"If you love only the people who love you, why
should you receive a blessing? Even sinners love
those who love them! And if you do good only to
those who do good to you, why should you receive
a blessing? Even sinners do that!"
Luke 6:32-33 [a]

We should look above and beyond, into all kinds of relationships, and at each of our surrounding circles: family, school, social life, work, and society. There are many encounters, contacts, and dealings happening in our day-to-day activities. We certainly deal with many people every day on many aspects of life. The student is dealing with the teacher and the employee is dealing with the boss. The car owner is dealing with the workshop mechanic, while our neighbours deal with each other. The big brother is dealing with his little sister, while the housewife is dealing with the handyman. The bus driver is dealing with the passengers, while the saleswoman is dealing with the customer. And at each encounter with anyone, we can make a positive impact if we start managing all the distrustful feelings.

A two-way impact

The positive impact we are talking about comes through different means. We can make a positive impact by educating moral behaviour, modelling of good manners, offering advice, teaching skills, developing talents, instructing a subject of interest, sharing experiences, or by writing an article for the church bulletin. Or simply by helping others reach their goals.

However, in our complex world, the hierarchy established within our societies, necessary to bring order, creates conditions prone for a predominantly unidirectional avenue to make any impact. But it is truly directional; we just have to wait for the opportunity to create the impact. Thus, the student can show the teacher his or her strong determination to learn; the employee can show the boss his or her creativity; or the parishioner can show the priest his or her deep repentance.

Watch out for negative impact

The second aspect to consider is that we could also make a negative impact, and just by being conscious of that notion can help us avoid it. If we are upset or annoyed by something, let's not take it out on the neighbour or someone else. If we are late for an appointment, let's not run over anyone who happens to cross our path. Moreover, we may think that, by doing nothing when we have the opportunity to do something, we are in neutral territory, since we are not creating any impact, neither positive nor negative.

Neutral impact does not exist. If we think it is neutral because it is neither positive or negative, then it is negative, simply because we are not giving any positive impact. We are walking on the sidewalk and someone comes in the opposite direction. He sees us, but we just ignore him. What a difference it would make if we just smile at him!

A chain reaction

The third aspect to keep in mind is that, many times, the impact received, whether positive or negative, can be transferred to a third person, in a cascade, provoking a chain reaction. Let's say we vent our frustration on a stranger. That, of course, will create a negative impact. And then this stranger could, in turn, vent his anger, created by the negative impact, on his family or someone else. What he received, he will now give, recreating the impact over and over again. Imagine the saleswoman being rude to her customer. The customer will leave without buying anything, and probably will go to a different shop in a defensive way; or go home and shout at her children for apparently no reason. If it is the other way around and the customer is rude to the saleswoman, the next customer will be attended to by a disgruntled saleswoman who may do a mediocre job, which in turn could annoy the shop manager. And so on. Now imagine that all starts with a behaviour that creates a positive impact; chances are then high that the impact remains positive all along.

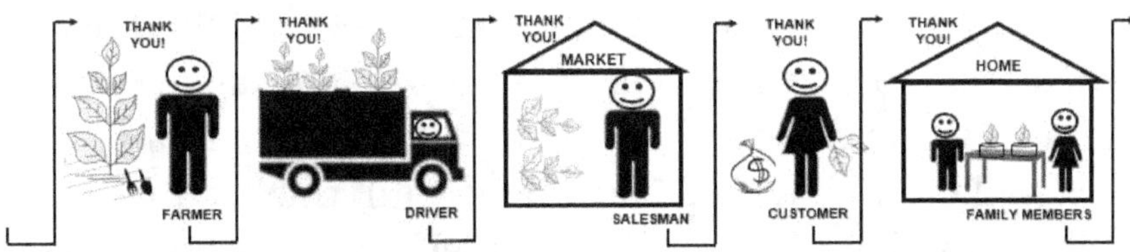

If someone thanks us for holding the door for him, we will likely thank the next person holding the door for us. If we smile to that person walking in the opposite direction, he or she will smile too, and may even keep it... A smile that the person coming from behind will also then receive.

Offering help

Helping someone creates a positive impact, definitely. We all know it. To offer help, we need to be proactive, committed, and sincere; but help has to be provided where it is needed and when needed, and most importantly, when wanted. This is why we also need to be cautious. If people don't want it, just leave it. It is better not to insist, since the person may become defensive, blocking out any possibility to make any impact; or rather, the impact could become negative, even on us. But if the help is well received, we feel happy, helpful, useful, fulfilled, and rewarded; all blessings. This is why we should, in turn, accept the help offered to us by someone.

Offering feedback

Feedback could be a powerful way to create an impact. When offering feedback, it has to be conveyed in an assertive way, showing genuine interest, care, and appreciation for that person, and a sincere and honest wish to help her.

There are times when we need to give a more delicate feedback, for example, when we need to highlight a wrongdoing to a friend, classmate, or a colleague. In this instance, we may begin with something positive about her, then explain the wrongdoing, and end the feedback with another positive remark about herself. We may or may not know the causes for such behaviour, but probably only the consequences of such behaviour or attitude. We should highlight them with assertiveness. Assertiveness should be used to help and not to accuse, as she could feel blamed or victimized, making her probably reject our feedback and, consequently, our help.

Small actions can make positive impact

Small actions can also make a huge positive impact, and many of these "small" actions are actions that you would like to see others make towards you as well.

> "Do for others just what you want them to do for
> you."
> *Luke 6:31 [a]*

We have opportunities to make small actions practically every day. For example, helping someone to carry a heavy load; or sharing your umbrella with others on a sunny or rainy day. If traveling on public transportation, we can give up our seat; also, we may allow those passengers exiting the train to step out first, before we proceed to get in. If we are driving, we may give way politely to others on the road; and perhaps offer someone the ride to the nearest train station. Noticing a tourist or strangers as being lost, we may offer help in giving them useful directions.

We could offer to pay the bus fare to someone struggling to find coins; and we could definitely hold the door for others when entering a building or an office. At the food courts, we could return our tray after the meal. We do this and would immediately see everybody else doing the same; it all becomes a cascade of blessings.

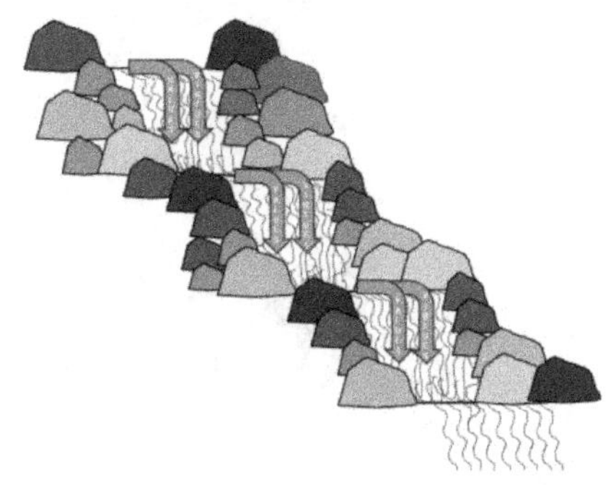

It is certainly a chain reaction of good thoughts, feelings, wishes, attitudes, and behaviours pouring out to all who surround us.

Modelling can make positive impact

We don't need to talk much to convey a message. We can create a positive impact by showing blessings and good manners by our own actions, by modelling. We show good manners by saying "thank you" and "please"; by eating without making a noise; by dressing appropriately when going to church; and by not spitting on the sidewalk. We show blessings when we pick up litter; or talk softly while on the train; by greeting the people already inside the lift; or by being punctual to our meeting.

How wonderful it would be to come to an old age and realize that we have taught others a multitude of good things, that we have impacted positively to so many people, and that we have contributed for a better society. We are all called to live a fruitful life and to leave a worthy legacy.

> "What you have done will be praised from one generation to the next; they will proclaim your mighty acts."
> *Psalm 145:4* [a]

TENTH PRINCIPLE

REVIEW YOURSELF CONSTANTLY

For so many things that we could do in a week, in a month, in a year, or our entire life, if we don't stop at some point to review what has been attached to our crosses, we will not know if we are living, or have lived, a life full of blessings.

"Let us examine our ways, and turn back to the
LORD!"
Lamentations 3:40 [a]

This is the personal evaluation of our thoughts, feelings, wishes, attitudes, and behaviours. We may call it an examination of conscience, or just self-examination for short. The frequency of such self-examinations would depend on each individual, but it would never happen if we are not conscious that we have a conscience that should be examined. Our self-examination should tell us how our growth journey has been progressing, and if we are moving in the right direction.

To be really successful, we need to assimilate deep inside all the blessings accumulated so far, in a way that behaving with integrity will be effortless with the passing of time. Once all that is imbibed, all our goodness will pour out from within. And having accumulated the many blessings, it means that no room has been left for curses. All that effort should have prevented us from making and tolerating many mistakes, much less failures.

However, making mistakes does not mean we don't progress somehow. On the contrary. For the person who doesn't make mistakes, it's because he doesn't move; and not moving is a mistake in itself. Everybody makes mistakes, and whether fast or slow, progress is anyway being made.

Measure

We measure to keep track of the things we do or care about, and this is a very easy task to do in the tangible world, as for example when we measure our weight or the distance we've run.

Thus, the student would know in how much time he finished his homework or his test; the saleswoman, how many pieces of clothing she sold; the teacher, how many students passed the exam; the priest, how many parishioners attended his mass; the material supply manager, whether she stayed within the budget; and so on. And when we measure again the following week, month, or year, we can then determine how much we have progressed in each of those things. But the progress is successful if it meets the established objectives and its requirements, such as time, budget, use of resources, etc.

Doing things right the first time

Taking more time, or using more resources in excess of those initially considered, let alone repeating the job, and we will be attaching headaches to our crosses. We must make every effort to complete any task or any job both correctly and successfully the first time we attempt to do it. Achieving it in such a manner already makes a positive impact.

Is it possible to measure blessings and curses?

Our behaviour is a reflection of our thoughts, feelings, wishes, and attitudes. If we think badly of a person, we may then dislike him, which in turn makes us wish him ill-fortune, and we end up behaving inconsiderately against this person. It started with our thoughts. We could then count the times we have behaved rudely, disrespectfully, or aggressively towards this person.

Negative thoughts and feelings, such as pride, envy or lust may be much harder to measure. But, in many cases, we will notice that they produce pain in our hearts, that we become irritable, and that we move away from people; certainly, our cardiovascular responses are indeed affected. But as challenging as it looks, it can be done. We might be able to "measure" the number and duration of these events.

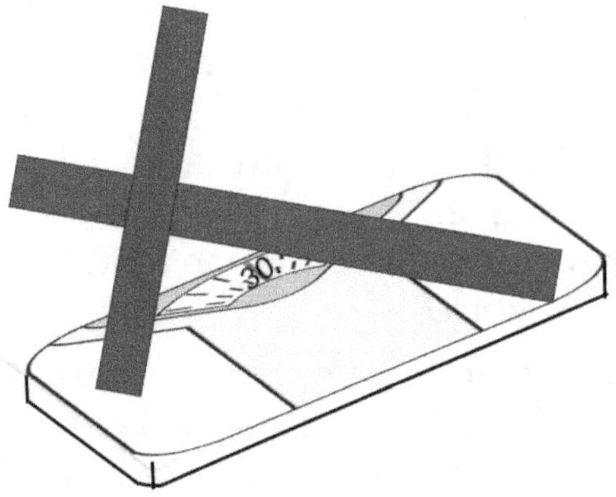

Is there someone still, who we don't want to forgive? Are there feelings of envy, resentment, vengeance, or hatred against someone? Do you wish that this person you hate would be dead? Am I lying more? Are there times when I am insulting my friends or strangers? Are we feeling distress or anxiety more often? Or impatient, pessimistic, rejected, or worthless?

> "A proud and avaricious man is never at rest; but
> a poor and humble man enjoys the riches of
> peace."
> *Thomas A Kempis, in 'The Imitation of Christ'*
> *Penguin Books*

We said before that by filling our time with blessings, we are leaving no room for curses; and the same happens vice versa. If we discover during our self-examination that we still have evil thoughts and feelings, meaning curses, we still have some work to do in order to continue progressing on our blessings.

How many hugs have I given today? Are those increasing or decreasing compared to last week? Have I given to charity more in the past 12 months than during the previous years? Am I spending more time with my parents or siblings than I did before? Have I smiled to at least two people today? Am I now more ready to make a small action of kindness? How many times did I read the bible this week compared to last week?

Measuring blessings to that level may be impractical for some, but the point to highlight here is that we must perform the self-examination regularly. At least, to ask ourselves if we now feel more at peace, relaxed, balanced, and happier; if so, that is a sign of progress. And knowing we have progressed will certainly encourage us to continue.

Reject vices

When carrying out our self-examination, another aspect to review is vices, a huge curse. Vices destroy our body, mind, and soul. Vices can bring other curses; we may end up cheating, stealing, lying, harming... or even worse. Vices cause us to become addicted, and addictions make us slaves.

Decades ago, it was quite normal to watch TV commercials about cigarettes and alcoholic beverages. Thankfully, many governments have realized the high costs incurred in treating and curing the people who have fallen sick because of these vices, so they have implemented laws that control and restrict their consumption. But the internet era has opened up, or made much more accessible, other vices like gambling, gaming, pornography, and black-market business dealings. And all can start with someone, a "friend", offering us a cigarette, a drug, or introducing us to gambling for us to fall into a vice.

Not that these vices didn't exist before, but the internet has made them much easier to access. That, together with the evil influence, make people fall, and falling into a vice is to become a prisoner; sometimes for life.

But with integrity, we can say "no" to that, firmly and resolutely. We do have the choice between the blessing and the curse.

> "Christ freed us to make us really free; so
> remain firm and do not submit again to the
> yoke of slavery."
> Galatians 5:1 [b]

Walk the talk

Integrity is to have all our thoughts, feelings, wishes, attitudes, and behaviours "in line", and driven by solid and unbreakable values as we have already said. But, during our life journey, when we are learning and growing, sometimes it is not like that. Our behaviour is not in line with our wishes, and these are not in line with our thoughts. This is where our integrity is compromised. Even if we, ultimately, behave correctly, that inconsistency would place us in a vulnerable position later on, and we could end up behaving dreadfully next time.

'We thought to cross over a red light when driving, but we stopped the car in time.' 'We encounter a rude person and felt like insulting him, but we controlled ourselves.' 'We thought to lie to our parents about the exam we had failed, but in the end, we told them the truth.' There are surely many examples when our thoughts were wrong but we end up doing the right thing.

'We felt like giving $20 to the beggar, but we gave him only $1.' 'We wanted to be closer to God, but never went to church.' 'We thought of spending the weekend with our parents, but in the end, we decided to spend it at home.'

Many examples when our thoughts are right but we end up behaving wrongly.

> "They claim that they know God, but their actions
> deny it."
> *Titus 1:16* [a]

All the above examples also happen, if seen vice versa, only to show our inconsistency or lack of alignment.

The more aligned our behaviour is to our thoughts, provided they are righteous, the more blessings will be accumulated during our growth journey. Once we get them aligned, the blessings will be embedded into our own nature and character, thus showing up naturally and spontaneously. If during our self-examination, we conclude that our behaviour is not in line with our thoughts, we need to be honest enough to acknowledge it, and then commit to continue working on our behaviour; otherwise we are only cheating ourselves. We have and need to walk with integrity. That is our responsibility.

> "For Yahweh gives wisdom and from his mouth
> come knowledge and insight. He reserves his help
> for the upright and is a shield for those who walk
> in integrity."
> *Proverbs 2:6* [b]

Our responsibility

We are truly responsible for our thoughts and actions, but sometimes we don't accept the responsibility, refusing to see it. We blame something or someone else for results arising from our own decisions and actions; we even dare to justify our improper actions. That, in the end, is being dishonest with ourselves. 'We never gave more than $1 to the beggar for being suspicious of what he would have done with the money; and not because of our lack of generosity.' 'We never went to church, blaming the lack of time, when it was simply because of lack of commitment... or faith.' 'We lied because our parents would have scolded us, should we have told the truth, and not because of our lack of respect towards them.' 'We didn't cross the red light for fear of being fined; not because we intend to be good citizens that respect the right of way of others.'

Each one of us may have a reason to behave differently, guided by the way we think. It is up to each one of us to make the examination of conscience, and to commit to work on our integrity. It is our responsibility. The truth is that, in many cases, our trials and tribulations are merely derived from our lack of commitment to strengthen our integrity.

Engage

The purpose of self-examination is to improve, to be a better person, and learn if we are using our resources wisely. It will allow us to correct our path as required.

Because time is indeed limited, and we don't know how much of that we have left, everything we do must be done according to our values and using our blessings right on the spot, without deviating from the illuminated path that leads us to life. Therefore, we have to engage ourselves, consciously and sincerely, for each action we make. It must be our commitment.

We need to go out and act on what we need to do, with the right attitude of behaving with integrity. But we have to engage fully and to do things that create value. If an action is not of any value to anybody, then it is just a waste of effort and time. The hermit may not be causing any harm to anyone, but he is not bringing any joy either.

We should never rest on our laurels. That is being submissive, and the submissive does not grow. The submissive is basically stuck in his journey, and at the end of his days, after having wasted his time, he will regret it. He would have lived an unproductive and unfruitful life, full of curses.

We are called to do much better than that. God has given us the potential. We just need to dive into life and do what we have to do. With unbroken values, solid blessings, and faith that God will keep us on the right path, we shall have a long and fruitful growth journey.

"Yahweh shall fill you with all kinds of good
things, increasing the fruits of your womb, the
fruits of your livestock, and the fruits of your land,
which Yahweh promised on oath to your ancestors
that He would give you."

Deuteronomy 28: 11 [b]

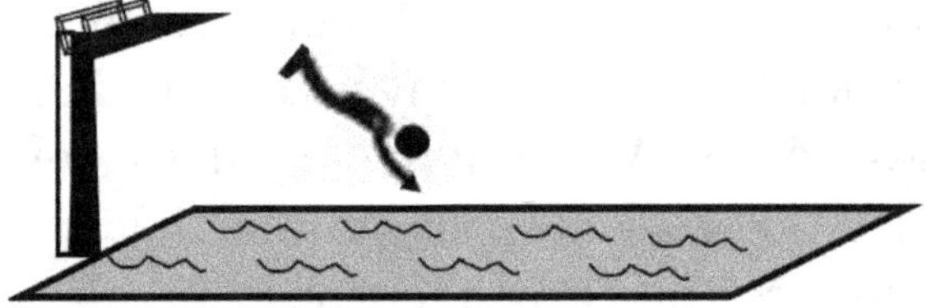

"Listen, my sons, to a father's instruction and pay attention so that you may gain insight. For I have given you good principles; do not discard my teaching!"

Proverbs 4: 1-2 [b]

NOTES

NOTES

NOTES

9 789811 433023